SPACE FACT FRENZY!

by Emma Carlson Berne

CAPSTONE PRESS
a capstone imprint

Published by Capstone Press, an imprint of Capstone
1710 Roe Crest Drive, North Mankato, Minnesota 56003
capstonepub.com

Space Fact Frenzy! was originally published as *Totally Wacky Facts About Planets and Stars*, copyright 2016 by Capstone Press.

Copyright © 2026 by Capstone. All rights reserved. No part of this publication may be reproduced in whole or in part, or stored in a retrieval system, or transmitted in any form or by any means, electronic, mechanical, photocopying, recording, or otherwise, without written permission of the publisher.

Library of Congress Cataloging-in-Publication Data is available
on the Library of Congress website.

ISBN: 9798875233920 (hardcover)
ISBN: 9798875233876 (paperback)
ISBN: 9798875233883 (ebook PDF)

Summary: There's a SPACE FACT FRENZY headed your way! Did you know that life on Earth wouldn't exist if the sun were any larger or any smaller? Or that the temperature on Mars can change more than 1,000 degrees Fahrenheit between day and night? Whether you are in the mood to browse or to devour a book in one sitting, dozens of bite-size facts and surprising photos will teach you all sorts of cool things about space!

Editorial Credits
Editors: Alison Deering and Chris Harbo; Designer: Tracy Davies;
Media Researcher: Svetlana Zhurkin; Production Specialist: Whitney Schaefer

Image Credits
Getty Images: Alex Teng, 19, Andrzej Wojcicki, 41, berkay, 7, dottedhippo, 32, DWPhoto, 63, leonello, 18 (middle), Melissa Ross, 43, Mimi Ditchie Photography, 17 (top), Science Photo Library/Mark Garlick, 8, 31, 37, 42, 44, 59, Science Photo Library/Mehau Kulyk, 14, Sciepro, 20, 58, StockByM, 53, Stocktrek Images, 51, Stocktrek Images/Alan Dyer, 29; NASA: ARC/Rick Guidice, 36, Johns Hopkins University Applied Physics Laboratory/Carnegie Institution of Washington, 33, JPL, 28; Shutterstock: agsandrew, 39, Alpha Factory Std, 17 (bottom), Andrii Iemelianenko, 5 (front), Artsiom P, cover (Jupiter), back cover, 1 (bottom), 34, 46, 48, 49, 64, AstroStar, 26, AvDe, 55, buradaki, 1 (top), 4 (middle), 16, CkyBe (speech bubbles), cover and throughout, Claudio Caridi, 23, 50, 52, david.costa.art, 54, Denis Belitsky, 11, Digital Storm, 24, Elena11, cover (Saturn), gn8 (rays and lines), cover and throughout, grey_and, 22 (middle), IkaPhoto, 6, IQ art_Design (arrows), cover and throughout, jaya diudara80, 38, joshimerbin, 47, kinziramtane, 10, Krzysztof Bubel, 18 (top), Luba Vega (space silhouettes), back cover and throughout, Lukasz Pawel Szczepanski, 21 (sun), ManuMata, 57, MattL_Images, 4 (left), Mel Gonzalez, 27, Mr.Music (sunglasses), cover, 21, muratart, 15, NASA images, 56, 62, nednapa, cover (top right), Nerthuz, 4 (right), 30, 45 (middle), Oleksandr Boiarin (shooting stars), cover and throughout, Photoongraphy, cover (Earth), Rawpixel, 5 (back), sasaperic, 13 (bottom), Sergey Fedoskin, 60, T.Thinnapat, 40, Thierry Lombry, 13 (top), Torontotokio, 21 (top), v_kulieva (gradient background), back cover and throughout, Vadim Sadovski, 25, van van, 12, Vibe Images, cover (top left), Vladi333, 35, 61, Wichaiwish, 22 (top), Yellow Cat, 45, Yukhym Turkin, 9

Any additional websites and resources referenced in this book are not maintained, authorized, or sponsored by Capstone. All product and company names are trademarks™ or registered® trademarks of their respective holders.

Printed and bound in the USA. PO 6307

An Out-of-this-World
Collection of Space Facts...............4

Unbelievable Universe......................6

Galactic Wonders.............................16

Incredible Inner Planets 30

Awesome Outer Planets 46

AN OUT-OF-THIS-WORLD COLLECTION OF SPACE FACTS

Are you fascinated by the mysteries of the universe and the secrets of our solar system? Do you want to know ABSOLUTELY EVERYTHING there is to know about them? Well, you've come the right place! This book is bursting with info about the big bang, sun burps, Martian mountains, and so much more. So don't wait another moment! Turn the page for a frenzy of space facts!

UNBELIEVABLE UNIVERSE

Many people believe that the universe exploded into existence during the big bang.

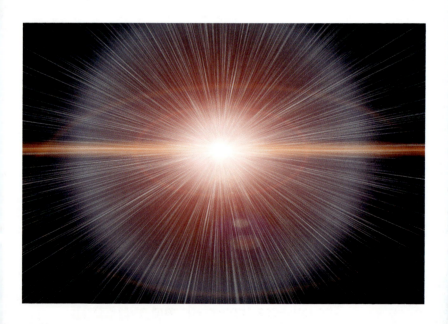

Before the big bang, the entire universe was the size of a pebble.

WOW!

The universe expanded from a tiny mass in a trillion-trillionth of a second.

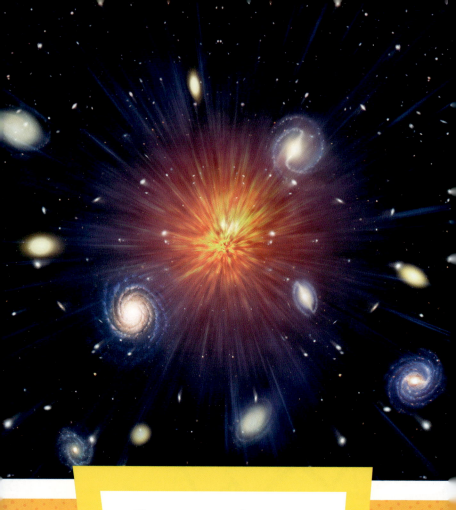

The universe isn't done growing—it's still expanding outward in every direction.

No one has figured out how big the universe is. It has no end, no edges, and no boundaries.

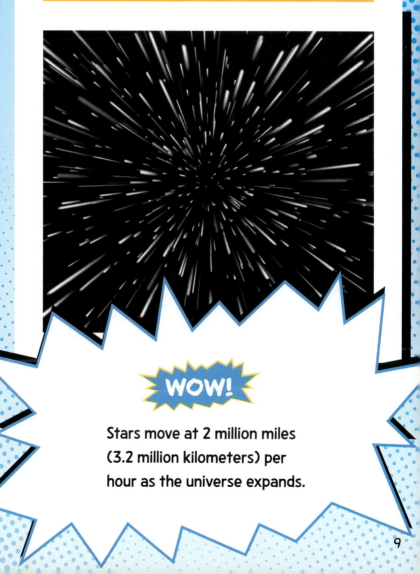

WOW!

Stars move at 2 million miles (3.2 million kilometers) per hour as the universe expands.

There are about a septillion stars in the universe—that's 10 followed by 24 zeros!

We can see only about 3,000 stars with our naked eyes.

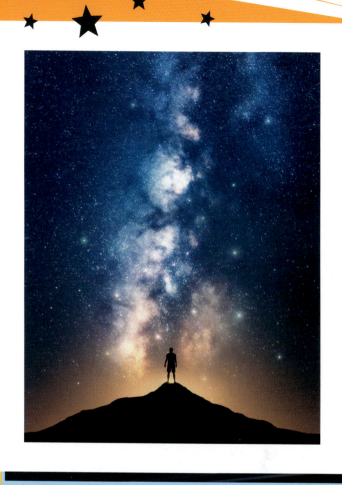

Some stars are as old as the universe itself—13.8 billion years.

When a huge star collapses, a black hole is created.

The gravity inside a black hole is so strong, even light can't escape from it.

WOW!

If you were in a black hole, your body would stretch out like a long piece of spaghetti.

Supernovas are giant explosions from the death of giant stars.

A supernova 25 light-years from Earth could wipe out most life here.

When a supernova explodes,
it can outshine an entire galaxy.

GALACTIC WONDERS

Some galaxies look like spirals, some like flat balls, and some have no particular shape.

You can see galaxies 2 million light-years away with the naked eye.

WOW!

Earth is in a spiral galaxy known as the Milky Way.

If our solar system were the size of a quarter, the Milky Way would be the size of North America.

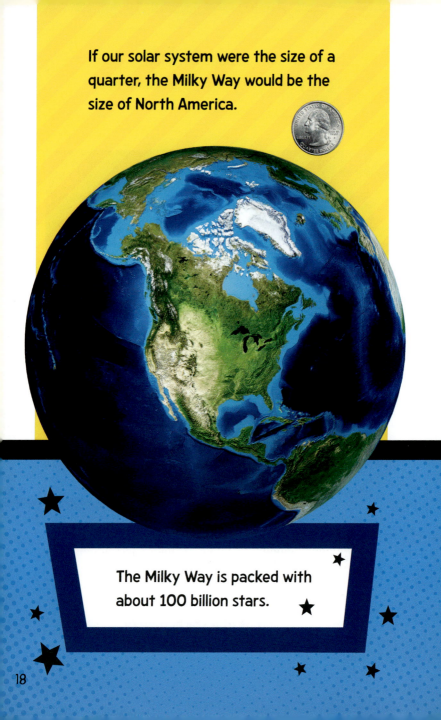

The Milky Way is packed with about 100 billion stars.

The biggest star in the Milky Way is 1,500 times bigger than the sun.

The sun makes as much energy as 100 billion tons (91 billion metric tons) of dynamite exploding every second!

The surface of the sun burps and boils like a pot of oatmeal.

WOW!

Solar flares shoot thousands of miles into space.

21

If the sun were the size of a basketball, Earth would be the head of a pin.

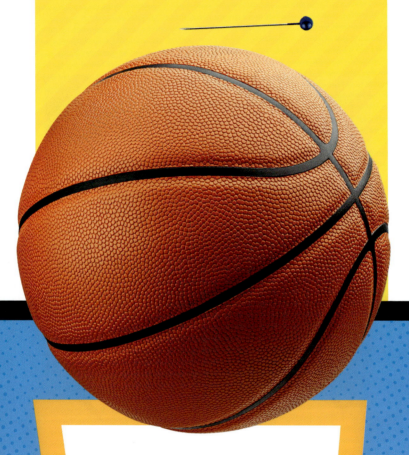

Life on Earth wouldn't exist if the sun were any larger or smaller.

When the sun finally dies, it will be crushed down to the size of Earth.

23

The sun's "gas tank" is about half full—it has burned through about half its lifespan.

A 100-pound (45-kilogram) person would weigh more than 2,700 pounds (1,225 kg) on the sun.

The sun's gravity keeps Earth from floating off into space.

Daylight looks like twilight during a solar eclipse.

The temperature on Earth can plunge 20 degrees Fahrenheit (11 degrees Celcius) during a total solar eclipse.

There are two solar eclipses per year somewhere on Earth.

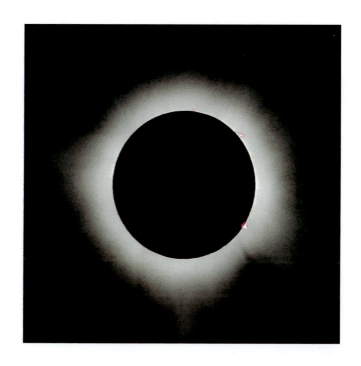

The eight planets that orbit the sun are Mercury, Venus, Earth, Mars, Jupiter, Saturn, Uranus, and Neptune.

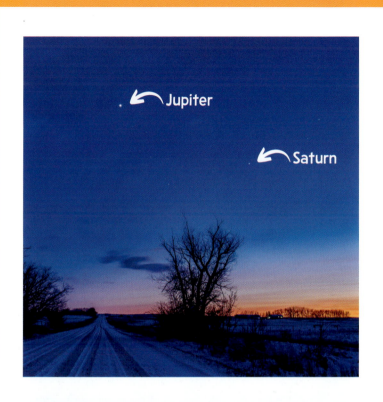

You can see all of the planets, except Neptune, in the night sky without a telescope.

29

INCREDIBLE INNER PLANETS

Mercury's temperature can change 1,090°F (605°C) between night and day.

Mercury has no wind, water, or atmosphere, which means it also has no weather.

WOW!

From Mercury, the sun looks three times larger than it does on Earth.

The stars move across the sky three times as fast on Mercury as on Earth.

Some cliffs on Mercury are 1 mile (1.6 km) high.

One crater on Mercury, Caloris basin, is longer than the state of California!

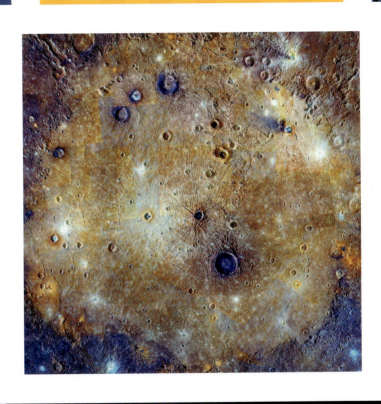

Venus is called Earth's sister planet. They are almost the same size.

One day on Venus equals 243 days on Earth.

When compared to the other planets, Venus rotates backward.

The temperature on Venus is hot enough to melt lead.

It rains acid on Venus.

WOW!

There is almost no light on Venus because thick clouds cover its atmosphere.

Earth rotates every 23 hours, 56 minutes, and 4 seconds—not every 24 hours.

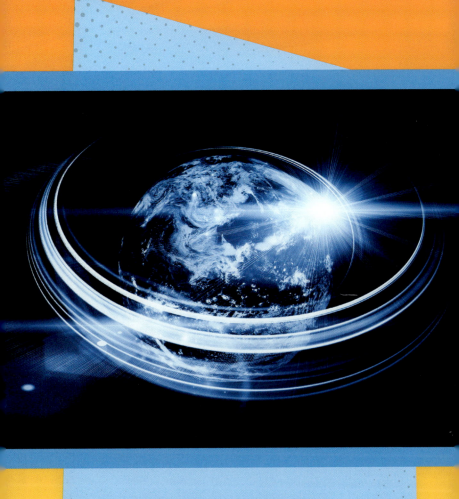

Earth's spin has slowed down 1.4 thousandths of a second in the past 100 years.

Beneath the thin crust of Earth's surface, molten rock roils and boils.

Earth's inner iron core is 9,000 to 13,000°F (4,982 to 7,204°C)!

The soil on Mars is RED because it's full of rust.

Most of Mars is red-colored, but there are patches of green soil. Scientists don't know why.

WOW!

If you weighed 100 pounds (45 kg) on Earth, you'd weigh only 37 pounds (17 kg) on Mars.

The tallest mountain on Mars is two-and-a-half times taller than Earth's Mount Everest.

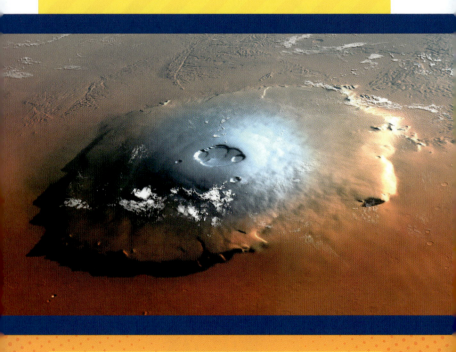

Mars has seasons like Earth, but they last twice as long.

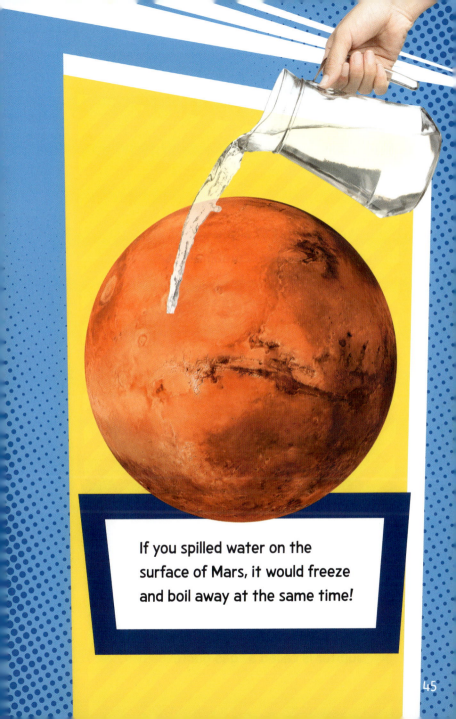

If you spilled water on the surface of Mars, it would freeze and boil away at the same time!

AWESOME OUTER PLANETS

Jupiter's mass is two-and-a-half times larger than that of all the other planets in the solar system combined!

Jupiter is called a "gas giant."

WOW!

Jupiter rotates so fast that the planet slightly flattens.

A day on Jupiter is only 9 hours and 55 minutes long!

One year on Jupiter equals 11.8 Earth years.

Humans could never live on Jupiter because it is covered in clouds of poisonous gas.

Jupiter has a large spot called the "Great Red Spot."

The Great Red Spot is a gigantic, swirling storm that is larger than Earth.

WOW!

The Great Red Spot is shrinking.

Saturn rotates once every 10 hours and 34 minutes. Its fast rotation makes Saturn the flattest planet.

WOW!

The clouds on Saturn are made of poisonous ammonia ice crystals.

Saturn is made mostly of gases—it would float if you could put it in a bathtub.

Saturn's rings are 186,000 miles (300,000 km) around, but only 0.5 mile (0.8 km) thick.

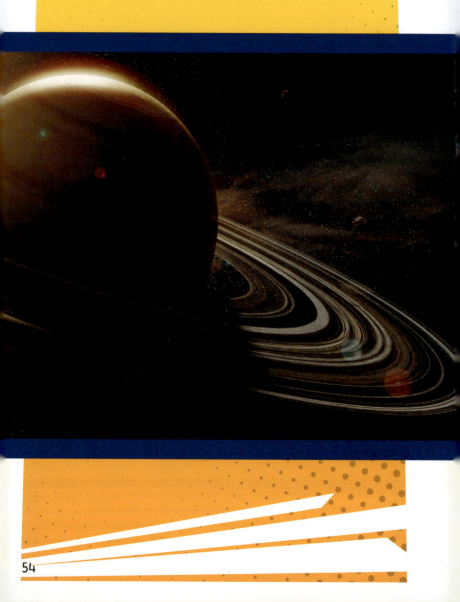

The rings on Saturn are made of chunks of ice and rock.

The chunks of ice in Saturn's rings can be as small as a grain of sand or as big as a house.

WOW!

Uranus is so far away from Earth, it would take about 9 years to get there in a spacecraft!

Saturn isn't the only planet with rings—Uranus has them too!

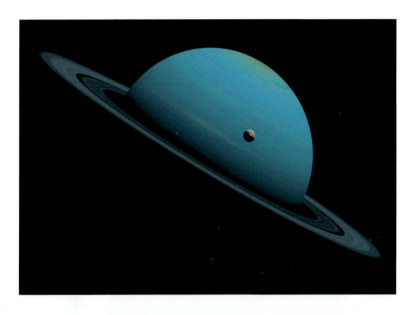

Uranus is called an "ice giant" because it's made up of ice and rock.

Uranus may have been hit by two massive objects, causing the planet to tilt on its side.

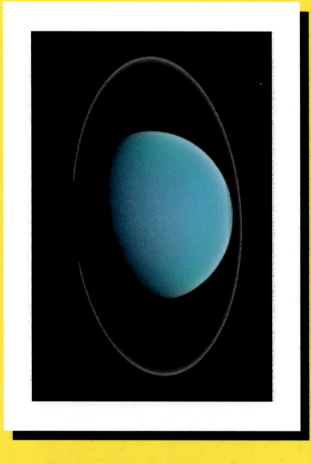

Because of its tilt, Uranus rolls like a barrel on its side.

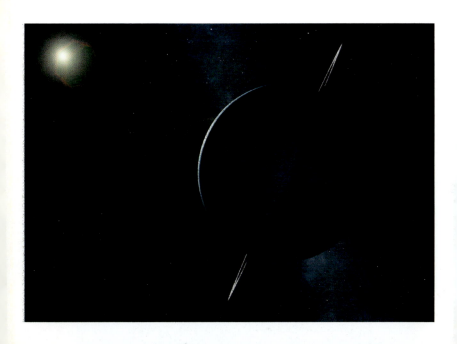

Uranus takes 84 Earth years
to go around the sun one time.

Neptune is made up of layers of gas but has a rock core.

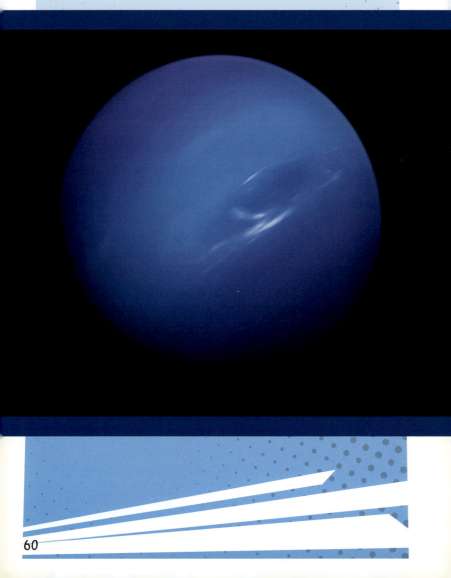

One year on Neptune is nearly 165 Earth years.

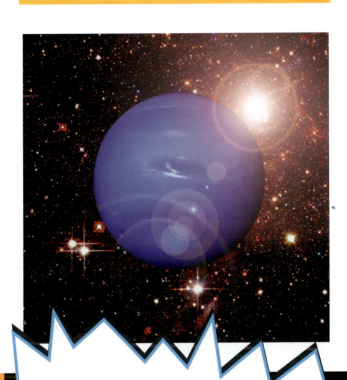

WOW!

Scientists think there might be an ocean of liquid diamond on Neptune's surface.

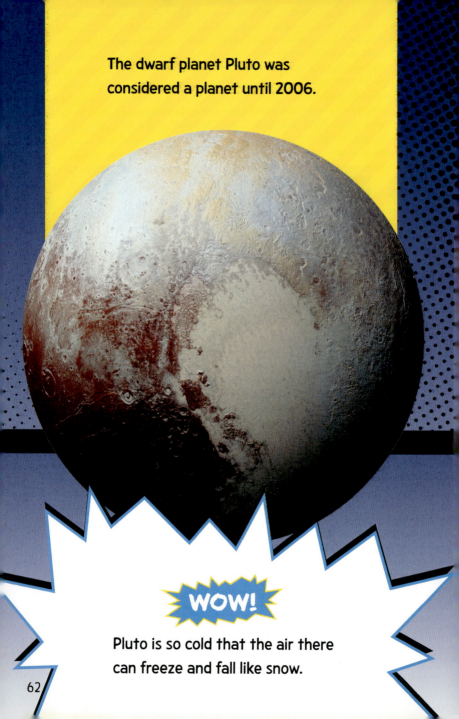

The dwarf planet Pluto was considered a planet until 2006.

WOW!

Pluto is so cold that the air there can freeze and fall like snow.

Dwarf planets are smaller than Earth's moon.

BOOKS IN THIS SERIES